P9-BBT-884

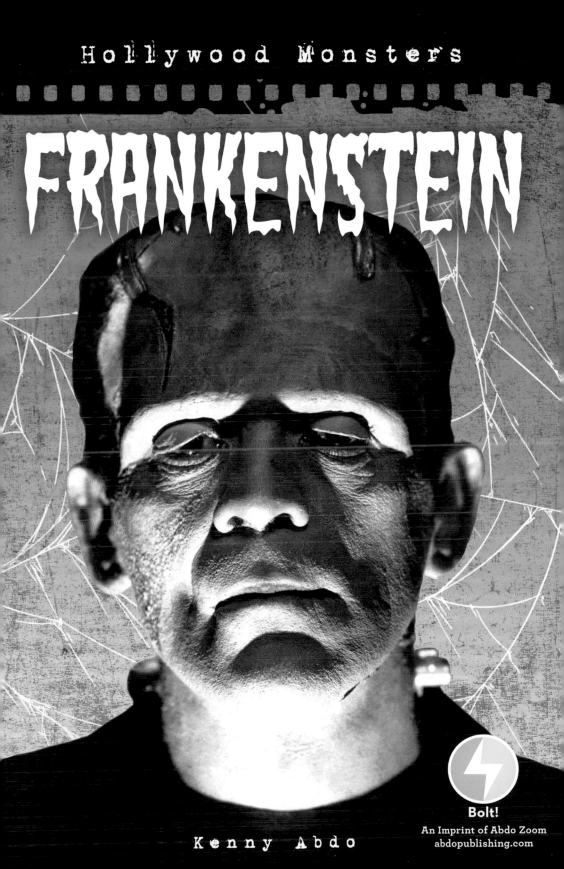

Hollywood Monsters

FRANKENSTEIN

Kenny Abdo

Bolt!
An Imprint of Abdo Zoom
abdopublishing.com

abdopublishing.com

Published by Abdo Zoom, a division of ABDO, P.O. Box 398166, Minneapolis, Minnesota 55439. Copyright © 2019 by Abdo Consulting Group, Inc. International copyrights reserved in all countries. No part of this book may be reproduced in any form without written permission from the publisher. Bolt!™ is a trademark and logo of Abdo Zoom.

Printed in the United States of America, North Mankato, Minnesota.
052018
092018

Photo Credits: Alamy, GettyImages, Granger Collection, iStock
Production Contributors: Kenny Abdo, Jennie Forsberg, Grace Hansen
Design Contributors: Dorothy Toth, Neil Klinepier

Library of Congress Control Number: 2017960601

Publisher's Cataloging-in-Publication Data

Names: Abdo, Kenny, author.
Title: Frankenstein / by Kenny Abdo.
Description: Minneapolis, Minnesota : Abdo Zoom, 2019. | Series: Hollywood monsters |
    Includes online resources and index.
Identifiers: ISBN 9781532123184 (lib.bdg.) | ISBN 9781532124167 (ebook) |
    ISBN 9781532124655 (Read-to-me ebook)
Subjects: LCSH: Monsters & myths--Juvenile literature. | Monsters in literature-
    Juvenile literature. | Monsters in mass media--Juvenile literature.
Classification: DDC 398.2454--dc23

TABLE OF CONTENTS

FRANKENSTEIN

Frankenstein is tale about a scientist who builds a creature out of old body parts. After bringing the monster to life, it terrorizes a village.

Frankenstein's monster is one of the most recognized **icons** in all of horror **fiction**.

ORIGIN

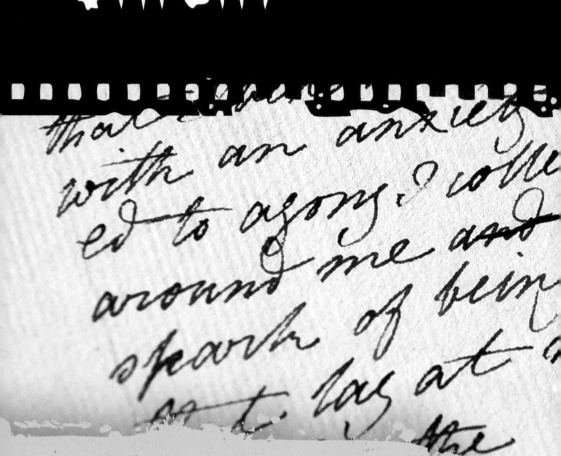

Mary Shelley wrote *Frankenstein* in 1814 as part of a contest with friends. She won at the age of 19.

nt of November ~~no while~~ ~~an~~ compleated; ~~and~~ ~~that~~ almost amount ~~ted~~ instruments of life ~~that I might~~ ~~endeavour~~ infuse a ~~m~~ to the lifeless thi~~s~~ feet. It was able~~ ~~morning, the rain ~~st the window ~~so~~nearly burnt out~~mer of~~ the half~~saw the dull yellow~~ It brea~~

FRANKENSTEIN.

"By the glimmer of the half-extinguished
light, I saw the dull yellow eye of the
creature open; it breathed hard, and a
convulsive motion agitated its limbs.
*** I rushed out of the room."

Page 43.

London, Published by H. Colburn and R. Bentley, 1831.

FRANKENSTEIN,

BY

MARY W. SHELLEY.

The day of my departure...

Frankenstein was published without Shelley's name in 1818. Critics bashed it as "horrible" and a "disgusting absurdity." It was reprinted in 1831 with her name to revived popularity.

HOLLYWOOD

In 1910, Thomas Edison made a 15-minute Frankenstein film. It is one of the first horror movies ever made.

Boris Karloff brought the
giant monster to life on the
big screen in 1931.

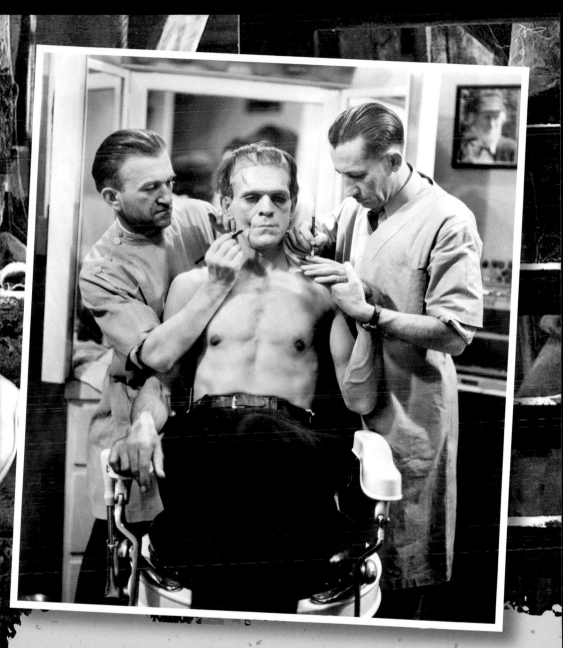

Karloff's makeup took four hours to apply each day. His costume weighed 48 pounds (22 kg). He also took out some fake teeth to give himself sunken cheeks.

The movie was so scary, it was banned in Kansas during its release. The **censors'** ruling was the film showed too much "cruelty" and **"debased** morals."

Still, the film was a giant hit!
It was the top movie at the US
box office in 1931.

LEGACY

16

The success of the movie lead to many **sequels** being made. In 1935, *Bride of Frankenstein* was released. It was even more popular than the original.

BASIL
RATHBONE
BORIS
KARLOFF
BELA
LUGOSI in

SON of FR

with
Lionel ATWILL

The story of the monster has influenced many films, television shows, and other spinoff works for more than a century.

The monster appears in the comedy *Young Frankenstein*, the hit TV show *The Munsters*, and the cereal Franken Berry.

GLOSSARY

big screen – another name for the movies.

censor – a person who removes material that is considered offensive.

debased – lowered in quality or value.

fiction – a story that is not fact.

icon – a person or thing regarded as a representative of something.

sequel – a movie, or other work that continues the story begun in a preceding one.

ONLINE RESOURCES

Booklinks
NONFICTION NETWORK
FREE! ONLINE NONFICTION RESOURCES

To learn more about Frankenstein, please visit **abdobooklinks.com**. These links are routinely monitored and updated to provide the most current information available.

INDEX